AT WAR WITH FRIENDS
ERIC TORGERSEN

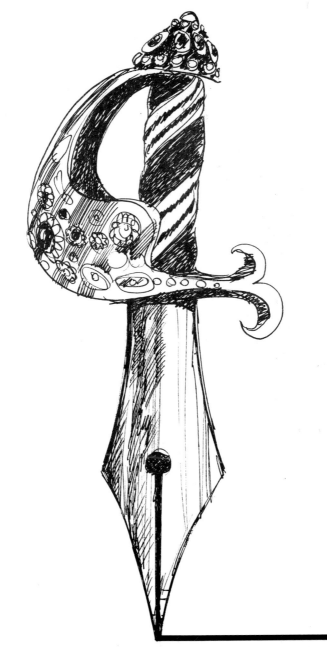

AT WAR
WITH FRIENDS

Eric Torgersen

an Ithaca House book

ithaca

AT WAR WITH FRIENDS

Grateful acknowledgement is due the editors of the following magazines in which poems from this book first appeared: *Back Door, Cimarron Review, Crazy Horse, Doones, Epoch, Greenfield Review, Happiness Holding Tank, Hearse, Kamadhenu, Nickel Review, Poems of the People, Salt Lick.*

ITHACA HOUSE
314 FOREST HOME DRIVE
ITHACA, NEW YORK 14850

for Paula

At War with Friends

CONTENTS

ONE

WHAT THE BLIND KID SAID

This is too easy
the blind kid said
who memorized cities
and did all he did
perfectly

If I could let go
of this cane
I could trip on a curbstone
get lost
have no address

If I could find
my eyes
I'd think about strangers
be frightened more
maybe not want
to touch things

If I could see
your face
I could trust you
hate you
say
you are beautiful

A WARNING

— the judge speaks

Conscience has mixed blood
he's a bastard

Conscience has no respect
he would take away your house

He shadows your daughter
down city streets

Will she marry Conscience
and a dark child come of it?

Conscience spits on the floor
speaks in whispers
can never be satisfied

Lock all the doors
he wants to enslave you like Hitler

THE MEETING

Tonight at the White Man's Society
a film about beauty and strength
in pale things:
clouds that vanish
(or gather, a black anger);
snowflakes that melt
(or gather);
water, in all its moods.

This room (green walls,
folding chairs) is the parlor;
they are the family here, together,
away from the strangers
who never apologize,
strangers proud
of their own strange sons.

They have family quiet here;
they sing in low voices
old songs;
fathers touch sons
who touch their rain-
pale sisters.

In the streets it's raining;
gangs of cars pass
the white letters: White Man's Society,
9:00 PM;
there are no dark faces
at the windows.

HOLLOWS

sustain us.

High and dangerous
rooms we look out of;

hollows of unknown
lives we break into.

Absent friends are
underground rivers—

hollows of all friends,
secrets we'd sleep in.

KILLING JENSEN

Make a life of killing
that weakling

who rests in delicate
moods like piles of pillows.

He's scared of everything:
snakes, razorblades, ladies.

He writes in a book of himself
that everyone reads.

He looks at his hands. He didn't hear
what you said.

Cut him open and step inside
or live, and he's dead.

HANDS THAT WRITE POEMS

tap table-tops.
Want language: a hammer, a knife.
Want an eye to obey.

Hands want to hold you
responsible;
don't want to beg.

Won't take your throat
on an order
(might take another's).

A book is no more
in the hands
than a rock or a stick.

This
is no house
hands are at home in.

ACCIDENTS

you're in every statistic
you hold millions of raffle tickets

accidents happen

parachutes, prophylactics,
seatbelts hideouts snakebite kits

know how to use them

if your traps catch rabbits
if you fall off your horse in the fox hunt

accidents happen

collisions, your sign, the laundromat,
friends of friends of acquaintances

know how to use them

avoid the right places, don't
dress for it, don't buy equipment

accidents happen

chain letters, free film, the weather,
subpoenas and songs on the radio

know how to use them

if parakeets keep in cages
but tigers are visitors

accidents happen
know how to use them

PICTURES: BIG SUR

Around the curve
(Highway 1)

a tall cop
slowing traffic,

a cycle sprawled
in high grass,

something covered
with a plastic sheet

except one black-
gloved hand

    *

The squirrel
far up
the redwood

falls
and falls,

crashes
in leaves
near our feet,

and tumbles
far down

11

(we listen)
the hillside

*

The pale green
and rose-
colored snake —

there
where I didn't
quite step —

glows
with its own
cold light.

*

Deep
in the National
Forest

in a glade
full of yellow
butterflies

drink
from your hands
at a spring

and think:
Viet Nam.

POET, MID-AIR

On the ground,
a yellow car,
trees,
friends' faces;

a woman
with a private look.

It would have to be
a good thing,

the poet's ascent,
ascension.

The sky
shifts clouds,
shifts colors;

planes
go places,
fast.

A good thing,
yes:

one more
nears the ground.

THE WICKED MESSENGER: ESCAPE-ARTIST

Escape
between voices—

go alone
on elec-
tronic plains

where roads
go everywhere

*

Friends' voices
calling

are arrows—
outrun them

*

Find silence
and sleep there

*

But won't you dream voices

voices

TWO

ETHIOPIA (STREETS)

UP EARLY: FIRST ETHIOPIAN MORNING

First weak
light,

white
Ethiopian
shapes

soon gone
in fog

    *

Rumble
& echo —

the lions
of the Conquering
Lion of Judah —

gone soon
in silence

    *

Morning
gone

in   sounds
in   sun

FERENJ : FOREIGNER

walks too fast
for all dignity,

fast as a porter
with a load

    *

walks stone paths
at night,

stops short
if a match flares

    *

says hello too much,
pays a fool's price,

looks beggars in the eye,
will not give

There are porters
(an out-caste)
for hire
cheap

but I carried
my suitcases
miles
in hot sun

to teach
the dignity
of manual
labor

as we
don't we?
know it
till a man

who wanted
I thought
doesn't everyone
here?

money
took them away,
would not
give them back

until
(but then,
smiling)

we'd arrived

and would not
I thought
won't everyone
here?

be paid.

I am a trained mechanic

angrier
I am a man

the man

who could make the jeep start
after the movie

offered fifty (Ethiopian) cents
demanding three dollars

said

and clung
for two blocks

to the jeep's locked back door
when we drove away

Why not?
gesture
with the rolled up
umbrella

if the taxi
swerved toward the puddle
to splash you

but later

not sidestep,
knock down
a child?

give an old priest
the finger?

FREE, WHITE,
TWENTY-ONE

(ON THE STREETS
OF AN OLD
OLD CITY)

Whores'
brown
arms,
brown
breasts.

*

Salesgirls'
legs,

stocking
grey.

*

Schoolgirls
in blue cloth,
grey cloth,
brown.

*

Such women
in black,

brown skin
gone rich

as dirt.

*

Free
in the streets

he trails
a widow

home.

Sitting on a rock
near the top of the hill
looking down.

You say: Hello.

He says: Everything,
house, cows, everything —
and you —*ferenj*—
say Hello.

THREE

LETTERS

JIM

We're so patient with you.
Everyone's interesting:

Dan's in Rome, should we hope
he'll come back? One friend's quietly

mad, no one knows it. You say
someone died, is he telling the story?

I know it's exciting: your big,
changing plans; knowing the names

of secretly famous poets. Hell, our just
plain bodies are funny predicaments

worth their weight in words.
But what if we listen, this once, to all

your talk, every last good intention.
It's late, very late, we've been drinking.

What if we say and you know
we mean it *Now more, tell us more.*

RALPH

Book after book
by our friends

these days: pleasure
I could get much

too fond of: the envelope
said you, my fingers

felt a book: the brain
said yours though I

knew better:
titles came, didn't

write them down
but I'll try again

(quick, no revision):
Fixin' to Die,

*Black Echoes, Ears
to the Wall, The Delicate*

*Armies, Sulfur,
The Innocent*: shit,

is that you
or me: thanks

for Taban's book
(did we

misuse *him*): send
yours—

soon—
or I'll end up

inventing it.

DENNIS, PUBLISHER

The book recedes
like an old

school friend
I don't see much

these days
though we stayed up

with wine
more than once

and matched
regrets:

you've been that
friend's lover

all along
so we're intimate

and embarassed:
he writes

love from you
and I write

love to:
we might

well stay
in touch

that way
for years.

DOUG

your typewriter
skipped

when I tried
to write poems there:

two steps
forward,

one back:
never does it

to you
so you say

but it did it
to me:

the signs
are all over

that poem
and I

can't erase them.

In a daydream
you called this

skinnypoetry,
littlemag work,

failure poems:
I called yours

success stuff,
New Yorker

verse:
after that

I don't know
what we said

but we left
feeling hurt, scared, alone.

DOUG, JACKIE: THE THEORY

Live
in this house
your way
every inch:
you do not
lack subjects.

Wear
and value
the tweed coat bought
second hand:
your crafts
perfect themselves.

Dine
with candles:
your readings
enchant.

Rescue
old things
and rescue
the small
day's poetries.

Live
in this town
every inch
and America
changes.

KIM: COUNTERCULTURE

one: *plastique*

needed a belt,
got cheap & got

plastic:
looks leather

from a distance:
my plastic gloves—

gifts—won't
wear well: shoes

come plastic:
my taillight

got busted, proved
plastic & it's

made in Germany.

two: quiz

the killer steps out
in the dead man's bright clothing:

is he singing?
fingerpopping? trucking?

does he limp still?
will he give some kid

up the street a nickel?
is he grinning, can he

barely keep from grinning?

three: capitals

they're swinging
their hips

in all
the world's

hip capitals,
Kim,

but that don't
mean they move

to the music.

DAVE: PARTIES

I want to say
oh
I could never do
party work:

what would they want
to eat:
how much beer:
what to say
to invite people:

I want to say
me
I'm a guest:
I tell jokes and speak
to the lonely:

But now
before heading

for her place
or mine

I want to take time out
to thank

those generous men
and women

who made this evening
possible.

THE POSSIBLE
BUSY MAN
SPEAKS:

FAIR THINGS
TO SAY
TO ANY FRIEND

IN THE FOG:

yes,
I'm doing
something easier,
doing it:

can't you
find something
to do
that you can do
and will do?

no?
that doesn't
seem fair to you,
does it?
what
will you do about it?

I'll do
what I can
to help;
in the end

though
it's yours to do
if it's to be done
at all:

that doesn't
do you
much good
but what more
do you
expect me to do?

I'm busy.

HELP

It's these in-
dividual-

ists & their
taste:

it's a going
to Europe scene:

I wanna
dance in a

circle some-
times but there's

all this good food 'n conversation.

FOUR

GOOD MOON

A priest was attacking the birth control ban and
the girl sitting next to me said to her friend, "Yeah,
they want us to *abstain*."

I sat on a bench in the town square of Quincy,
Illinois reading *Allen Ginsberg in America*.

Two little kids in the back of a big
Chrysler station wagon flashed us the V.

VISITING OLD FRIENDS / HITCHHIKERS

Too much to say
to say much.
There are kids to show, poems,
beans from the garden,
good places to swim;
we drink, smoke, keep smiling.
But kids cry, wives are so new,
there's someone someone doesn't know.

The hitchhikers will talk:
I'm learning to make artificial limbs.
The French in Quebec won't speak
to you in English. Flint's OK,
the freaks are together.

Goodbyes are all apology
and promise: Christmas?
We touch more now and kiss wives,
wave and wave.

What did we think
to get back? How unhappy we were,
how free, when we were new friends?
How we turned heads,
back when the light struck us perfect?

The hitchhikers say what's important:
A girl I met last summer is in Toronto.
I'm going to school in Chicago

in the fall. I live here,
it's OK, the freaks are together.

Say goodbye quick, good luck,
there are places to get to
and look, cars coming.

POET AND TEACHER

He lets his hair grow a little,
he says he *understands*,

he lends us books, lends us
words for why we should sleep together;

if his letter to John's Local Board
didn't really make sense,

if he wasn't much help
when they got Tim for dealing,

we *understand*:
we know he's all heart, he's a good head,

we know his hands are tied.